W9-ALJ-000

HUMAN BODY SYSTEMS

The Human
Nervous System

By Cassie M. Lawton

Cavendish Square

New York

Published in 2021 by Cavendish Square Publishing, LLC
243 5th Avenue, Suite 136, New York, NY 10016

Copyright © 2021 by Cavendish Square Publishing, LLC

First Edition

No part of this publication may be reproduced, stored in a retrieval system, or transmitted in any form or by any means—electronic, mechanical, photocopying, recording, or otherwise—without the prior permission of the copyright owner. Request for permission should be addressed to Permissions, Cavendish Square Publishing, 243 5th Avenue, Suite 136, New York, NY 10016. Tel (877) 980-4450; fax (877) 980-4454.

Website: cavendishsq.com

This publication represents the opinions and views of the author based on his or her personal experience, knowledge, and research. The information in this book serves as a general guide only. The author and publisher have used their best efforts in preparing this book and disclaim liability rising directly or indirectly from the use and application of this book.

Portions of this work were originally authored by Heather Moore Niver and published as *The Nervous System (The Human Body)*. All new material this edition authored by Cassie M. Lawton.

All websites were available and accurate when this book was sent to press.

Library of Congress Cataloging-in-Publication Data

Names: Lawton, Cassie M., author.
Title: The human nervous system / Cassie M. Lawton.
Description: First edition. | New York : Cavendish Square Publishing, 2021.
| Series: The inside guide: human body systems | Includes index.
Identifiers: LCCN 2019058113 (print) | LCCN 2019058114 (ebook) | ISBN
9781502657312 (library binding) | ISBN 9781502657299 (paperback) | ISBN
9781502657305 (set) | ISBN 9781502657329 (ebook)
Subjects: LCSH: Nervous system–Juvenile literature.
Classification: LCC QP361.5 .H86 2021 (print) | LCC QP361.5 (ebook) | DDC
612.8–dc23
LC record available at https://lccn.loc.gov/2019058113
LC ebook record available at https://lccn.loc.gov/2019058114

Editor: Kristen Susienka
Copy Editor: Nathan Heidelberger
Designer: Deanna Paternostro

The photographs in this book are used by permission and through the courtesy of: Cover S K Chavan/Shutterstock.com; pp. 4, 28 (top) Sebastian Kaulitzki/Shutterstock.com; p. 6 StockSmartStart/Shutterstock.com; pp. 6-7, 20 CLIPAREA | Custom media/Shutterstock.com; p. 8 Designua/Shutterstock.com; p. 9 VectorMine/Shutterstock.com; p. 10 Hein Nouwens/Shutterstock.com; p. 11 BlueRingMedia/Shutterstock.com; p. 12 Rido/Shutterstock.com; p. 13 Inegvin/Shutterstock.com; p. 14 Aliona Ursu/Shutterstock.com; p. 15 Alila Medical Media/Shutterstock.com; p. 16 Silbervogel/Shutterstock.com; p. 18 KateStudio/Shutterstock.com; p. 21 Cassiohabib/Shutterstock.com; p. 22 Ezume Images/Shutterstock.com; p. 24 © CORBIS/Corbis via Getty Images; p. 25 Daxiao Productions/Shutterstock.com; p. 26 (left) Katrin Kaemper/Shutterstock.com; p. 26 (right) SARIN KUNTHONG/Shutterstock.com; p. 27 Monkey Business Images/Shutterstock.com; p. 28 (bottom) TijanaM/Shutterstock.com; p. 29 (top) Andrii Vodolazhskyi/Shutterstock.com; p. 29 (bottom) The world of words/Shutterstock.com.

Some of the images in this book illustrate individuals who are models. The depictions do not imply actual situations or events.

CPSIA compliance information: Batch #CS20CSQ: For further information contact Cavendish Square Publishing LLC, New York, New York, at 1-877-980-4450.

Printed in the United States of America

Find us on

CONTENTS

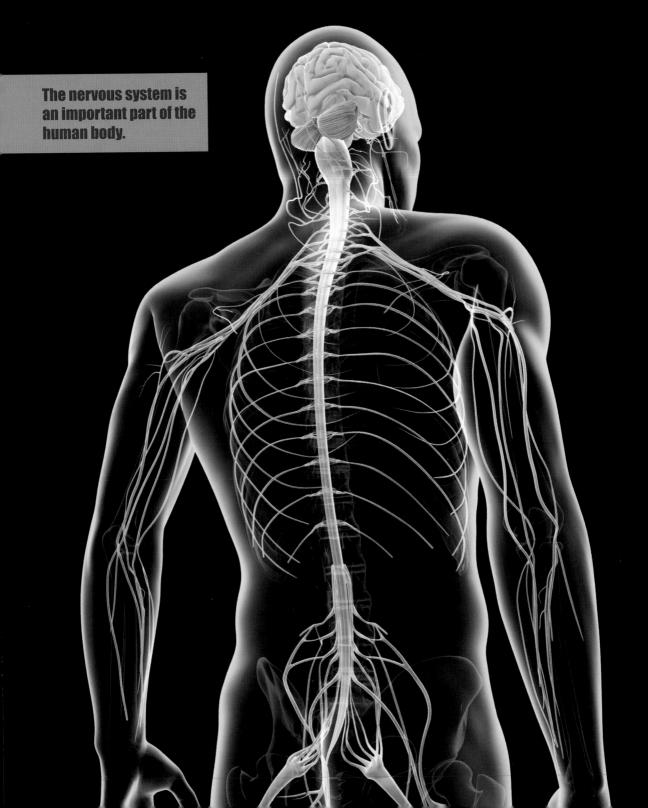

The nervous system is an important part of the human body.

WHAT IS THE NERVOUS SYSTEM?

Chapter One

Your body works through the help of many different networks, or systems. Each system has a different job. One system controls oxygen in your blood. Another makes sure your food is digested and removes waste from your body. The nervous system carries messages between your brain and the rest of your body. These messages can include if food is hot, if it's cold outside, or if you should fight an enemy or run away.

How Does It Work?

You feel the warm sun on your skin and taste cold chocolate ice cream on your tongue. These are examples of your nervous system at work. You use your five senses—sight, hearing, touch, smell, and taste—constantly. They give you information about what's happening around you. This information speeds through your nervous system, which is made up of the brain, spinal cord, and nerves, all the time.

The nerves send messages to the brain. The brain then decides what to do and tells the body how to act. This happens when your body tells you it's cold and you decide to put on a sweater. You also need your nervous system to do things such as read, eat, sleep, run, laugh, and even remember. You can't do much without your nervous system!

TWO DIFFERENT TYPES

The nervous system has two parts. The first part is called the central nervous system. It's made up of the brain and spinal cord. The central nervous system is the main part of the network. It's responsible for functions like thoughts, awareness, speaking, and being able to remember things from long ago. The second part is the peripheral nervous system. This system concentrates on the periphery, or outer edges, of the nervous system. Different nerves, **neurons**, and fibers outside the brain and spinal cord form the peripheral system. The peripheral nervous system carries messages from other parts of the body to the brain, and vice versa. The two parts of the nervous system work together. They also are constantly talking to each other to make sure the body is working correctly.

Fast Fact

On average, the spinal cord is around 18 inches (46 centimeters) long and 0.75 inches (2 cm) thick.

The nervous system is connected to your five senses, shown here.

TASTE

HEARING

TOUCH

SMELL

SIGHT

A Computer in Your Body

All the parts of the nervous system work together. Your brain is like your body's central computer. It controls nearly every single action and reaction you have—and it does this in almost no time at all.

Fast Fact

On average, an adult has about 0.5 cups (118 milliliters) of cerebrospinal fluid.

Your spinal cord is like a highway along which messages speed to and from the brain. The spinal cord is a long rope of nerve tissue that runs from the base of your brain down through the spine. Along the way, various nerves branch out and extend throughout your entire body. These nerves make up the peripheral nervous system.

The brain and spinal cord have a lot of important work to do, so the body has some ways to protect them and to make sure they stay healthy. Your skull protects your brain, and **vertebrae** are armor for the spinal cord. Layers of membranes called meninges and a clear liquid called cerebrospinal fluid provide some padding too. Cerebrospinal fluid also keeps the nerves healthy.

Keeping Things Running

The nervous system's two parts, the central nervous system and your peripheral nervous system, help you do things like remember and speak and also carry messages throughout your body, but what part of your nervous

The brain is at the center of the central nervous system.

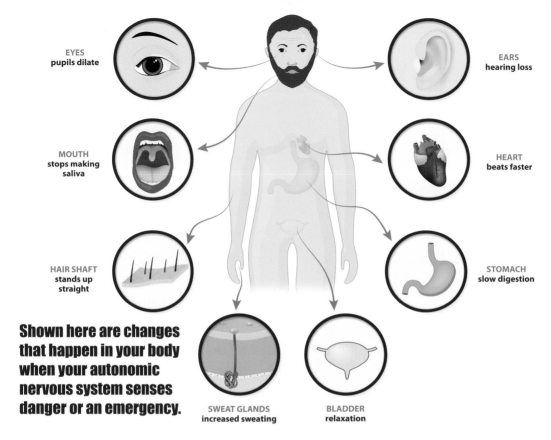

EYES
pupils dilate

EARS
hearing loss

MOUTH
stops making
saliva

HEART
beats faster

HAIR SHAFT
stands up
straight

STOMACH
slow digestion

**Shown here are changes
that happen in your body
when your autonomic
nervous system senses
danger or an emergency.**

SWEAT GLANDS
increased sweating

BLADDER
relaxation

system controls things like your breathing, heartbeat, and emotions? Your peripheral nervous system has a part called the autonomic nervous system. This system regulates some body functions without you having to think about them.

The autonomic nervous system is divided into two major parts: sympathetic and parasympathetic. Sympathetic nerves prepare your body to react to an emergency, such as freezing cold conditions or an injury. They also kick in when your body's internal chemistry is out of balance. Parasympathetic nerves keep your body running when it's at rest. These two types of nerves sometimes work against each other, but they also balance one another out. Another, minor part of the autonomic nervous system is the enteric nervous system. It's a group of nerve fibers that control actions in the **gastrointestinal tract**.

Fast Fact

Humans have 31 pairs of spinal nerves.

Sympathetic nerves help your body adjust to the world around you, such as when you sweat in hot weather. When you face a threat or a difficult new challenge, the whole sympathetic nervous system kicks into high gear. Your lungs work harder and your heart pounds faster so your blood can bring more oxygen to your muscles. That way, you're ready to face the problem or quickly run for safety. This is called the "fight-or-flight" response.

Peripheral Nerves

In the peripheral nervous system, there are two more groups of nerves besides autonomic. Spinal nerves originate in the spinal cord. They contain bunches of motor and sensory fibers. Each connects the spinal cord to a certain part of the body. Motor fibers send information from the central nervous system to the muscles. Sensory fibers carry information from skin, muscles, joints, and internal organs to the spinal cord.

Cranial nerves join parts of the brain to sense organs in your head, like your eyes and ears. They also connect to muscles, internal organs, and **glands** in the head and upper body. Cranial nerves are hard at work when you chew and then swallow food. They also help you blink.

PERIPHERAL NERVOUS SYSTEM

The peripheral nervous system (*in blue*) is made up of autonomic, spinal, and cranial nerves.

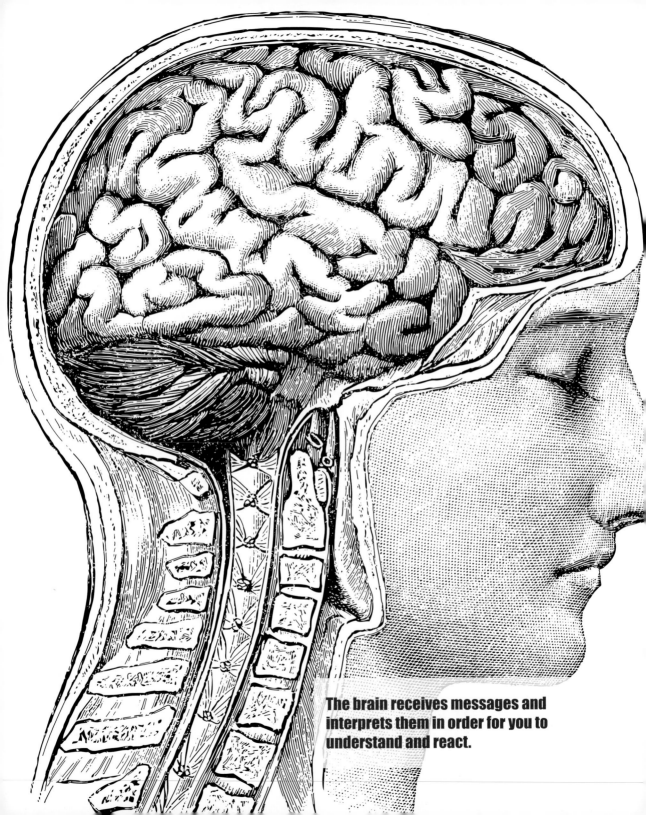

The brain receives messages and interprets them in order for you to understand and react.

WHAT ABOUT THE BRAIN?

Chapter Two

The brain is the center of the nervous system. Without it, people couldn't function properly. It's made up of three sections: the forebrain, midbrain, and hindbrain. The forebrain is the biggest and most complicated part. It's mainly made up of the cerebrum, which contains the information that gives each of us a personality—emotions, intelligence, and memory. It also allows us to feel and move around.

The cerebrum is divided into two halves, or hemispheres. The right half controls the left side of the body, and the left half is in charge of the right side of the body. A band between the two parts, called the corpus callosum, helps them communicate.

Each hemisphere has four areas, which are called lobes, that are responsible for different kinds of information storage

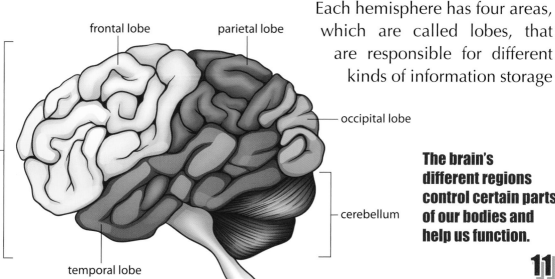

frontal lobe

parietal lobe

occipital lobe

cerebrum

cerebellum

temporal lobe

spinal cord

The brain's different regions control certain parts of our bodies and help us function.

11

Fast Fact

On average, 90 percent of people in the world are right-handed, meaning they use the left side of their brain to write.

and activities. The four lobes are the frontal, the parietal, the temporal, and the occipital lobes.

We need our brain to write the answers to math problems in school.

Inner Parts

The outer layer of the cerebrum is called the cortex, or gray matter. It collects information from your five senses and then sends that information to other parts of the nervous system. The thalamus, hypothalamus, and pituitary gland make up the inner part of the forebrain. The thalamus receives information from sensory organs and passes it to other parts of the brain. The hypothalamus regulates body processes that occur automatically, like body temperature. It also controls the pituitary gland, which is involved in growth.

The midbrain is below the middle of the forebrain. Its chief job is to manage the messages sent between the brain and spinal cord. Finally, the hindbrain sits below the back of the cerebrum. It's made up mainly of the cerebellum. The cerebellum helps you balance and move.

Together with the midbrain, parts of the hindbrain (called the pons and medulla) make up the brain stem. The brain stem's **role** is to receive, send out, and organize all the brain's messages. It's a little like the brain's

THE BRAIN'S TWO SIDES

The cerebrum's two hemispheres look a lot alike, but they do more than control different sides of the body. The right side of your brain controls sensitivity and creativity. The left side controls logical and objective thoughts. It used to be thought that people were "right brained" or "left brained." People who were "right brained" were said to like singing, dancing, writing, or reading more than math. People who were "left brained" were thought to enjoy more logical subjects, like science or statistics. However, people don't agree with that thinking anymore. Studies have shown that there is no such thing as "right brained" or "left brained." Nearly everyone is "brain ambidextrous," or able to use both sides of the brain equally.

Although "left brained" and "right brained" are terms of the past, this diagram shows ideas or processes associated more with the left and right sides of the brain.

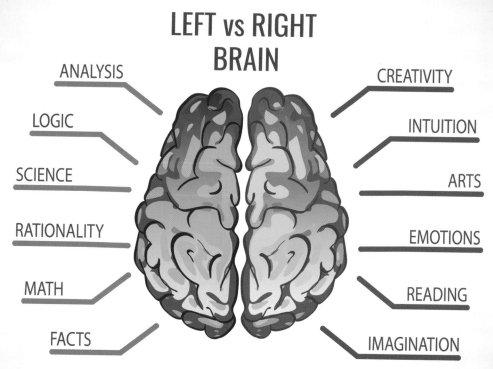

LEFT vs RIGHT BRAIN

ANALYSIS

LOGIC

SCIENCE

RATIONALITY

MATH

FACTS

CREATIVITY

INTUITION

ARTS

EMOTIONS

READING

IMAGINATION

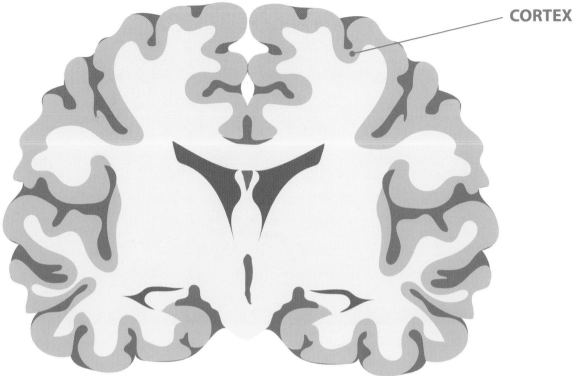

CORTEX

secretary. It's also the part of the brain that helps with some of those actions that happen without any thought, like swallowing and breathing.

The cerebrum's gray matter, or cortex (in dark peach), covers the brain.

Supporting Parts

At the base of your brain is a tiny structure called the pituitary gland (or hypophysis). Are your clothes getting too small? You can thank your pituitary gland! It makes and releases special **hormones** to make your body grow. It's also responsible for releasing

Fast Fact

The cerebellum is a part of the hindbrain. Its name comes from the Latin words for "little brain" because it looks like a small cerebrum.

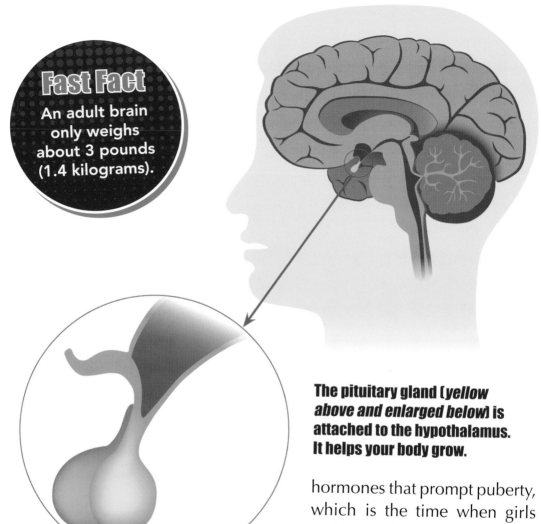

Fast Fact

An adult brain only weighs about 3 pounds (1.4 kilograms).

The pituitary gland (*yellow above and enlarged below*) is attached to the hypothalamus. It helps your body grow.

hormones that prompt puberty, which is the time when girls and boys develop into women and men. The pituitary gland also works with other glands to do things such as control the sugar and water in your body.

Your hypothalamus is near the pituitary gland. It produces hormones that control many things, such as body temperature, mood, thirst, hunger, and even the release of hormones from other glands.

NEURON

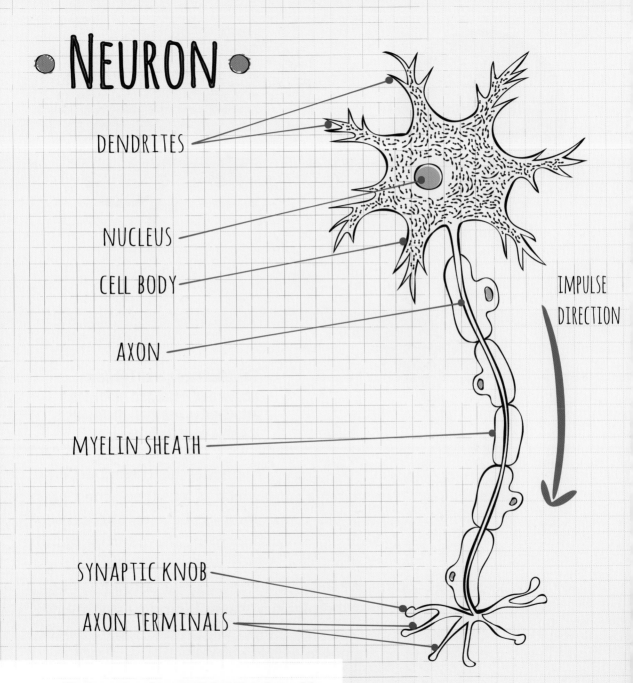

DENDRITES

NUCLEUS

CELL BODY

AXON

MYELIN SHEATH

SYNAPTIC KNOB

AXON TERMINALS

IMPULSE DIRECTION

Neurons may be small, but they have big responsibilities inside the human body.

HOW IT ALL WORKS

The nervous system works as a unit inside the body. Its main operators are the brain and spinal cord, but other elements play **crucial** roles too.

Navigating Neurons

Nerve cells, called neurons, are big heroes within this system. Neurons are shaped like flat, stretched stars. Many are less than 0.04 inches (1 millimeter) long, but some can be more than 3 feet (0.9 meters) long.

When you see, smell, taste, and feel sticky strawberry jam, your sensory neurons send that information to your brain right away. Motor neurons from the brain carry information telling your body to swallow the jam, clean it off your fingers or face, and maybe even reach for more jam.

Neurons have four main parts: the cell body, axon, axon terminals, and dendrites. The cell body is much like the cells in other parts of your body. The axon is a long, thread-like part that carries electrical messages, or impulses. The branched ends

Fast Fact

Your brain contains about 86 billion neurons, and they're so small you need a microscope to see them.

of axons, called axon terminals, send information to other neurons. Dendrites are branch-like parts that reach out toward other neurons to receive information.

Synapses

When you're born, you have all the neurons you'll ever have. However, they don't have connecting pathways at first. Your brain makes them as you learn.

As you grow, your neurons are constantly trading information. One neuron may form connections with 5,000 to 200,000 other neurons!

Synapses, shown here, help messages move throughout the body.

Fast Fact

Your skin has more than 4 million sensory receptors, which take in information about touch, temperature, and pain. Most of them are in your fingers, tongue, and lips.

These connections are called synapses. Each one has a tiny axon terminal from one neuron and tiny dendrite from another reaching out to each other.

Neurons have two kinds of synapses. Electrical synapses, or gap junctions, are physical connections between two different neurons. They allow electrical impulses to pass freely from one neuron to another. Chemical synapses, or synaptic clefts, are spaces between the axon terminal of one neuron and the dendrite or cell body of another. When an electrical signal reaches the axon terminal, the terminal releases a special chemical that crosses the synaptic cleft. The dendrite of the other neuron receives the chemical message and turns it back into an electrical impulse. This pattern continues until the message reaches its destination.

Brain Change

Did you know that your brain is changing all the time? You have billions of neurons that help you learn. As you learn more, the messages move between neurons over and over again. Once you do something enough, your brain notices patterns and creates pathways between the neurons to make things easier.

Think about how hard it can be to learn to do something new, like swimming. At first, it can be really hard to remember how to move your arms and legs in the water, not to mention when to breathe without

THE EMOTIONAL AMYGDALA

Emotions are a big part of being human. People get upset, show happiness, and are sad at certain times in their lives. Emotions are controlled and processed in your brain. A part of the brain called the amygdala plays a big part in emotions. It's a little cluster of cells on either side of your brain. The word "amygdala" means "almond," which is exactly what these clusters look like. The amygdala is often associated with strong emotions like fear or love. The cell clusters of the amygdala form part of another system in the body, which is called the limbic system. The limbic system deals with emotion, motivation, and behavior. It's also found in other animals aside from humans.

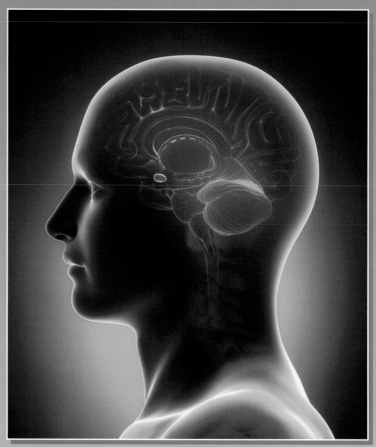

Do you feel happy, sad, or scared? The amygdala, shown here, is most likely involved in those feelings!

Fast Fact

Neurotransmitters are chemicals released at the end of a nerve fiber. They help transfer a message between neurons.

The brain is constantly learning! That's why it takes time to get better at a new skill, such as swimming.

taking in water. However, it's important to keep trying and practicing when you're learning something new. As you practice kicking and paddling more, your neurons send the same messages again and again. Eventually, your brain creates a "swimming" pathway, and soon you can swim easily!

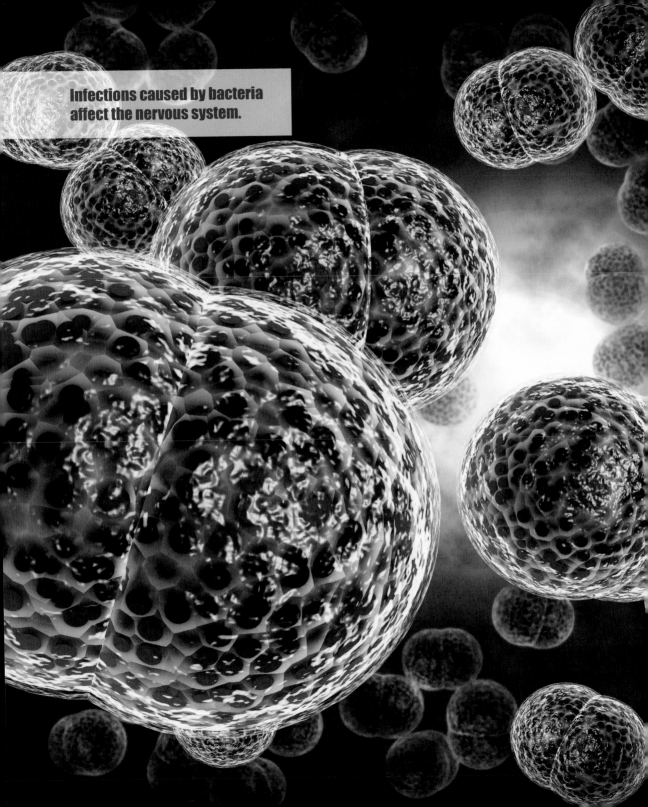

Infections caused by bacteria affect the nervous system.

BRAIN AND NEURON ISSUES

Your body is a **complex** structure, and it sometimes needs help to keep working properly. Sometimes a part of it stops working entirely. Your nervous system can be affected by an injury or **infection** that can stop your body from working as it should.

Problems with the nervous system can show up as little changes in personality or more serious symptoms, or signs, like blindness. They can even lead to death. Some problems are hereditary, or passed from parent to child, while others result from an infection or injury. Some have cures, while others don't. Doctors who help with nervous system **disorders** are called neurologists.

Infections

Infections in the body can cause meningitis, which is an inflammation, or swelling, of the protective membranes of the brain and spinal cord. Shingles, or herpes zoster, can occur in someone who has been infected with the chicken pox virus. It attacks the nerve endings and causes a rash on the skin. Tetanus is a disorder caused by bacteria found in soil and manure. It attacks the nervous system and causes a tightening of the muscles.

President Franklin Delano Roosevelt, shown here, lived with a disorder that affected his nervous system.

Diseases

There are many diseases associated with the nervous system, but some are more well-known than others.

In the 1900s, a disease called polio affected many people around the world. This disease targeted motor neurons. Symptoms of polio included sore muscles, especially in the arms or legs, back or neck pain, headaches, and muscle spasms. One person who was believed to have suffered from polio was President Franklin Delano Roosevelt, although studies now think he may have had a different condition that affected his nerves. In the 21st century, polio has been almost completely eliminated around the world.

Multiple sclerosis (MS) cripples the central nervous system. It's called a demyelinating disease because it breaks down the myelin sheath, a layer that wraps around your nerve cells to protect them. If the myelin sheath is damaged, nerve fibers can't work correctly. The **immune system** plays a part in MS. Certain **white blood cells**, part of the body's natural defense system, attack the myelin as if it were an enemy. MS is the most common demyelinating disease, and its cause is unknown. Medications and physical therapy can help while scientists search for a cure.

Fast Fact

Actress Selma Blair has suffered from multiple sclerosis for years. She announced she had the disease in 2019.

24

Exercise is an important thing to do if you want to stay healthy!

Another serious nervous system disorder is Alzheimer's disease. It breaks down and kills the brain's cells. This affects the brain's ability to remember. People who have Alzheimer's tend to be older, and many of them forget family members, friends, or key events in their lives. Some medicines help, but there's no cure.

Fast Fact

Bananas have lots of potassium in them. Dairy products like milk and cheese are good sources of calcium.

Fight Disease, Stay Healthy

How can you keep your brain and nervous system healthy? There are lots of ways! You should always eat a healthy diet with lots of foods containing potassium and calcium. These minerals help your nervous system function properly. Also, go out and play! Exercise that's good for the rest of your body is also good for your nervous system.

Life would be pretty dull without a nervous system. Without this complicated network of brain, spinal cord, and nerves, you couldn't communicate with your friends, draw, or play sports, and what fun would that be? Your heart wouldn't beat, and you couldn't breathe. Actually, you couldn't even exist!

OTHER NERVOUS SYSTEMS

Any animal that has a backbone has a nervous system similar to ours. Such animals are called vertebrates, and they include fish, birds, reptiles, amphibians, and other mammals. Generally, they have a brain and spinal cord that do a lot of the "heavy lifting." They also have a peripheral nervous system that carries messages between the brain and spinal cord and the rest of the body.

Invertebrates—animals that don't have a spinal cord—have different kinds of nervous systems. Many invertebrates have a nerve net, or a system of nerve cells and fibers that are distributed across the body like a net. For example, the jellyfish has a nerve net but no brain. The sponge doesn't have a clear-cut nervous system at all.

It's hard to believe, but the coral animals you see in the sea have a nervous system too! They don't have a brain, but they do have a basic nerve net. The net reaches from the coral's mouth to its tentacles. Some corals even have simple senses, like taste and smell.

Jellyfish and birds both have a nervous system, but they're very different.

It's important to keep your brain safe, especially while doing certain activities, like biking.

You can help keep your nervous system in good working order if you exercise, eat well, and follow important safety steps, such as wearing a helmet when you ride a bike. Now that you know how much goes on inside your brain, how will you best keep it safe?

Fast Fact

In 2018, over 850 people died while riding their bicycles on busy roads in the United States.

Jobs in the Brain

This chart explores different parts of the brain and activities they do every day.

Part	Activity
amygdala	processes emotions like fear or love
brain stem	receives, sends out, and organizes the brain's messages
cerebellum	responsible for balance, movement, and muscle function
cortex	collects information from the senses
hypothalamus	produces and manages hormones
thalamus	receives information from sensory organs
pituitary gland	controls growth and puberty

THINK ABOUT IT!

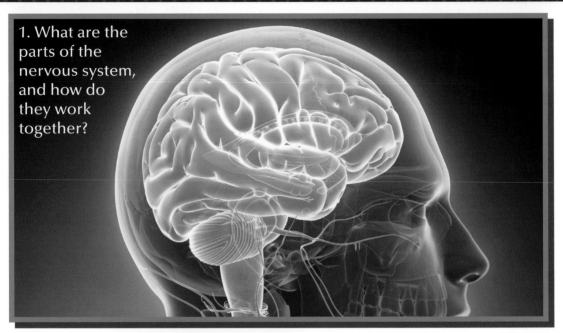

1. What are the parts of the nervous system, and how do they work together?

2. Imagine you're feeling sad or scared. What part of the brain is telling you to feel that way? What can help you feel better?

3. Why do you think it's important to have a healthy nervous system?

4. What activities can you do to help your nervous system stay helathy?

GLOSSARY

complex: Difficult to understand; made up of many parts.

crucial: Very important or needed.

disorder: A physical or mental condition that is not normal.

gastrointestinal tract: Also called the digestive system, the system in the body through which food moves and is broken down.

gland: An organ in the body that makes and releases hormones.

hormone: A chemical made in the body that tells another part of the body how to function.

immune system: The parts of the body that fight germs and keep the body healthy.

infection: The spread of germs inside the body, causing illness.

neuron: A single nerve cell. Neurons work together to carry electrical impulses between the body and brain.

role: A part someone or something plays; a responsibility.

vertebrae: The ring-shaped bones that make up the spine.

white blood cell: Part of the immune system that fights diseases.

FIND OUT MORE

Books

Gomdori Co. and Hyun-Dong Han. *Survive! Inside the Human Body, Volume 3: The Nervous System*. San Francisco, CA: No Starch Press, 2013.

Hansen, Grace. *Nervous System*. Minneapolis, MN: ABDO, 2018.

Terrazas, April Chloe. *Neurology: The Amazing Central Nervous System*. Austin, TX: Crazy Brainz, 2013.

Websites

Brain and Nervous System
www.hopkinsallchildrens.org/Patients-Families/Health-Library/HealthDocNew/Movie-Brain-Nervous-System
This animated video explains the different parts of the brain and their functions.

DK Kids: Brain and Nerves
www.dkfindout.com/us/human-body/brain-and-nerves
Check out this interactive website that explains the brain and nerves in the body.

Your Brain and the Nervous System
kidshealth.org/en/kids/brain.html
Learn about the brain and the nervous system at this website.

Publisher's note to educators and parents: Our editors have carefully reviewed these websites to ensure that they are suitable for students. Many websites change frequently, however, and we cannot guarantee that a site's future contents will continue to meet our high standards of quality and educational value. Be advised that students should be closely supervised whenever they access the Internet.

INDEX